'How it works'

THE COMPUTER

by DAVID CAREY
with illustrations by B. H. ROBINSON

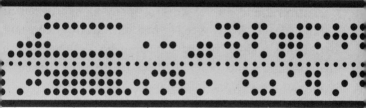

Publishers : Wills & Hepworth Ltd Loughborough

First published 1971   ©   *Printed in England*

What are Computers?

There is something about computers that is both fascinating and alarming. They are fascinating when they are used in rocketry and space research and when they enable man to get to the moon and back. Many people think of them as almost-human machines with 'brains' that allow them to think. After all, there are computers which play 'music' or 'speak'. On the other hand, we are inclined to be alarmed by their complex mechanisms and the involved scientific principles upon which they are built.

In fact, computers do not have brains and they cannot really think for themselves. They are primarily machines for doing arithmetic. They are automatically controlled and do the work of many human beings at fantastically high speeds, but the really important thinking is done by the humans who feed them with information and *program* them to perform particular operations with the information they are given.

Although primarily a calculating machine, the modern computer can also store up a vast mass of information. It can be programmed to carry out 'logical' operations, such as transferring certain information from one part of the machine to another, sorting this information and comparing it with other pieces of information or using it in arithmetical calculations. We hope this book will help you to understand how most of this is done.

4

0 7214 0286 0

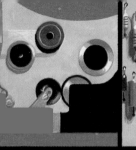
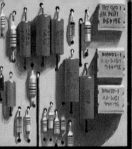

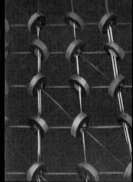

How Computers Developed

To think that computers have suddenly arrived on the scene would be wrong, although it is true that their number and use have greatly increased during recent years. Desk calculators have been in use for a very long time, and even in the days of the old navigators and astronomers there was a need for some sort of calculating instrument to relieve the human brain of work.

The first mechanical calculator was produced by Blaise Pascal in 1642. Others tried to improve on it but not until the nineteenth century was any real progress made. In 1801 a Frenchman named Jacquard invented a punched card system for controlling the threads on his weaving looms. Charles Babbage followed in 1833 with his 'Analytical Engine', which could perform calculations automatically, using punched cards. This was the first *digital* computer (see next page). The American Hollerith system also used punched cards, but the calculating machinery was operated by electro-magnetic means. It was introduced in 1889 and was generally used, in a highly developed form, right up to the widespread introduction of electronic computers in the 1950's.

1943 saw the need for computing artillery firing charts, and ENIAC (Electronic Numerical Integrator and Calculator) was born. EDSAC (Electronic Delay Storage Automatic Calculator) was first used at Cambridge University six years later. And so the modern electronic computer came into being.

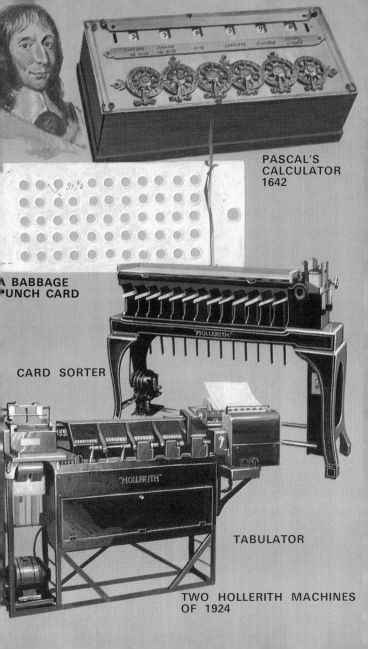

PASCAL'S
CALCULATOR
1642

A BABBAGE
PUNCH CARD

CARD SORTER

TABULATOR

TWO HOLLERITH MACHINES
OF 1924

Different Designs

The name computer, covers many different types of machine. They can be mechanical, electro-magnetic, fluidic or electronic, and can operate on either *analogue* or *digital* information; hence the names *Analogue Computer* and *Digital Computer*. This seems to introduce a complication right at the beginning, but there is no need to worry; we are only concerned here with the electronic digital computer.

Mechanical and electro-magnetic machines have working parts, i.e., numbered wheels that revolve and rods that move backward and forward to operate the mechanism. The electronic computer has no working parts as such, the whole system being operated by electricity.

An analogue computer is one in which a calculation is represented by a mechanical action such as the revolving of a wheel, the sliding of a rod or the variation of a voltage. A digital machine performs calculations with 'digits' (whole numbers or parts of numbers).

Computers are usually designed for a particular purpose, therefore each type of machine has its own variations, depending on the work it will have to do. Machines handling data for scientific work, for industry or for commercial undertakings, all have their own special features. In the following pages we will consider what we might loosely call a typical electronic digital computer system with its subsidiary equipment for receiving, storing and presenting information.

A SMALL DIGITAL COMPUTER
DESIGNED FOR THE BUSINESSMAN

A LARGE COMPUTER INSTALLATION

Data Processing

As we have already mentioned, there are a great many kinds of computer, each being designed for a particular purpose. Our 'typical' machine will very likely be used for 'data processing' in a large manufacturing organisation in which there will be a great amount of routine office work. For instance, the payroll has to be prepared every week and the names and wages of all the employees printed on their individual pay slips. Records of all the employees must be maintained and continually brought up to date as some people leave and others are engaged.

This computer may also be used to calculate the amount of material of different kinds that will be needed in factory production, and thus help to bring the hundreds of parts forward to the assembly line in the right sequence and at the right time. Records of sales of different products can be kept and forecasts made of possible future sales.

Organising the operations of a big factory with all its vital functions is a very complicated business, but a computer of the Advanced Data Processing (A.D.P.) type can be of immense help in providing the necessary information in a tiny fraction of the time it would take a large staff of clerical workers.

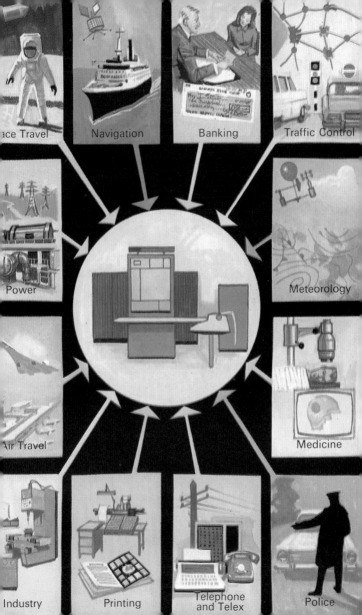

Space Travel

Navigation

Banking

Traffic Control

Power

Meteorology

Air Travel

Medicine

Industry

Printing

Telephone and Telex

Police

The Main Parts of a Computer

A computer system consists of several different units which each have their own special function.

Input Unit. This 'reads' the information to be stored in the machine and converts it into an electrical form which can later be used in arithmetical calculations.

Store. Data (information) can be permanently stored away here, usually in the form of recordings on magnetic material. It contains the vast mass of data a computer can deal with.

Registers. These are small stores. They hold the data to be worked on in a calculation and give it up as instructed. Data can be transferred from one register to another.

Arithmetic Unit. The actual operational unit where the calculations are performed and where the logical processes of selecting, sorting and comparing of information take place.

Control Unit. All the computer functions are co-ordinated by this unit, which interprets and carries out the instructions contained in a program.

Output Unit. This presents the results of a computer operation, very often in printed form as on a pay slip, or on magnetic tape, disc, drum or card, or even on a television screen.

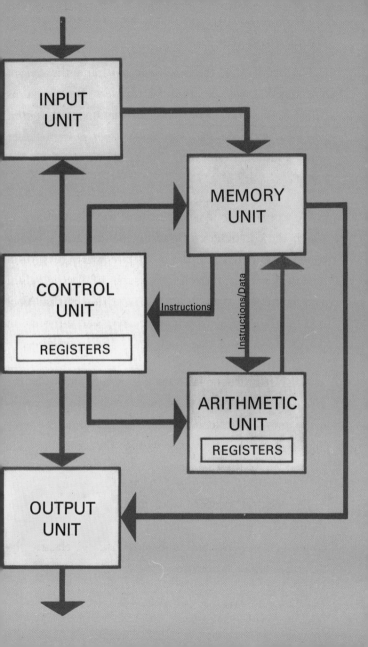

Combining the Parts

The main *store,* the *arithmetic unit,* and the *control unit* together with a group of *registers,* form what is called the *central processor.* Surrounding the *central processor* we have the *input* and *output units* together with additional storage. These are known as the *peripheral units.*

We can now see in a very general way the method by which the computer works. Information in a specially coded form is fed into the input unit where it is 'read' by a device which turns it into a series of electric pulses. The computer then 'writes' down this information, that is, transfers it to a *storage unit.* The information that is stored is of two kinds, data and instructions.

A list of instructions forms a *program,* and when the program is started data is transferred into the arithmetic unit and calculations are carried out at a very high speed. All activities within the computer are supervised by the *control unit.*

The central processor is made up from several thousand transistors together with other electrical components. Peripheral units are usually electrically-driven, mechanical devices.

INPUT

CARD
PUNCH

CARD
READER

MAGNETIC
TAPE

MAGNETIC
DRUM

MEMORY

CENTRAL
PROCESSOR

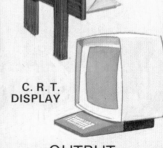

PRINTER

C. R. T.
DISPLAY

OUTPUT

The Computer Code

Human beings are able to recognise each other's handwriting and read the information that is written. They can also understand the spoken word. The same message can be given in any number of different ways by different people. But a computer, not having a brain, must have the information fed into it in one particular way—by a number or letter code.

The code that the computer understands is normally put onto cards or paper tape, through which small holes are punched in specially arranged patterns. A given pattern of holes punched down one column of a card or across the width of paper tape represents a particular character, that is, a letter or a number. The punching is done by an operator working a keyboard similar to that of an ordinary typewriter.

The speed at which the coding can be done depends on the speed at which the operator can work. This is not much more than five characters a second—too slow to be fed straight into the computer, which can 'read' the code very much faster than this. What usually happens is that a whole lot of cards, or a length of tape, are first coded on a machine away from the computer and later fed into the computer when there is enough information for the machine to work on at high speed.

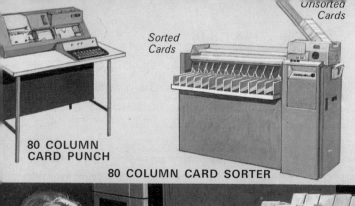

80 COLUMN CARD PUNCH

Sorted Cards

Unsorted Cards

80 COLUMN CARD SORTER

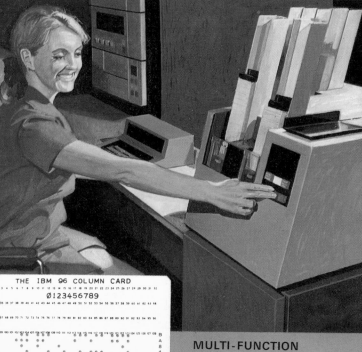

THE IBM 96 COLUMN CARD

Ø123456789

MULTI-FUNCTION CARD UNIT
Punches and sorts 96 Column cards

A 96 COLUMN CARD
(Slightly reduced)

IBM 3700

'Reading' the Code

Cards or paper tape with their punched holes are placed in the input unit of the computer. Here, the computer's reading mechanism translates the patterns of holes into electric pulses.

Punched cards may vary according to the design of the computer for which they are made. They are oblong in shape and usually divided along their length into eighty columns, each column having a possible twelve punched hole positions. Reading may be done with light, as with paper tape (see below), but another way is to pass the cards between a roller conducting electricity and a series of tiny wire contacts. Where the holes appear the contacts momentarily touch the conductor and an electric pulse is flashed into the machine. Where there is no hole there will, of course, be no electric pulse produced; thus the coded pattern is turned into a series of pulses and no-pulses.

Paper tape can be up to an inch in width. Again, different computers are designed to deal with different codes and there are either five or eight holes in a row across the width of tape, and usually ten rows in every inch of tape length (see diagram opposite page 34). When the tape is fed through the input unit it is read by a beam of light directed onto it. This shines through the punched holes and strikes a layer of photo-electric cells which turn the light dots into electric pulses.

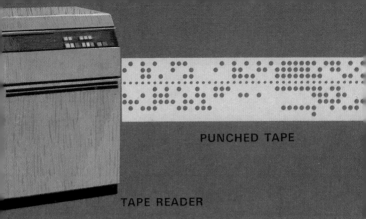

PUNCHED TAPE

TAPE READER

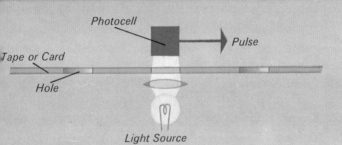

READING THE TAPE OR CARD

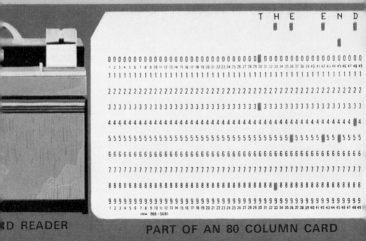

RD READER

PART OF AN 80 COLUMN CARD

Recording Information on Magnetic Tape

Feeding information into the computer by means of punched cards or paper tape is a well-tried method and not too expensive. Another material sometimes employed is magnetic tape, the recording process being similar to that used in ordinary tape recorders.

Magnetic tape has several advantages: it is much stronger than paper, the information can be packed in very tightly and is more easily prepared, errors can be more easily removed and the material is better to handle than cards or paper. Perhaps one of its greatest advantages is that out-of-date information can be wiped off the tape which can then be used again.

In the type of machine illustrated opposite, magnetic tape is held in cartridges, each cartridge containing 100 feet of tape. The information is recorded in the form of magnetic spots which are arranged in patterns representing characters, in a way similar to that in which the characters on paper tape are represented by patterns of punched holes. When the tape is run through the machine, its surface comes almost into contact with the reading/writing heads, a series of tiny coils with which information can be recorded (written) or played back (read). The speed of writing depends on the speed at which the operator can work (see page 16). Reading is done at the rate of 900 characters per second.

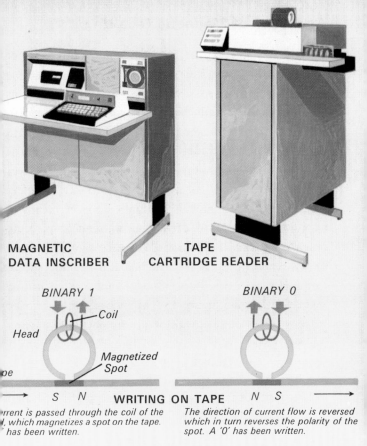

MAGNETIC DATA INSCRIBER

TAPE CARTRIDGE READER

BINARY 1

Coil

Head

Magnetized Spot

pe

S N **WRITING ON TAPE** N S

rrent is passed through the coil of the
, which magnetizes a spot on the tape.
' has been written.

BINARY 0

The direction of current flow is reversed
which in turn reverses the polarity of the
spot. A '0' has been written.

BINARY 1

BINARY 0

− +

+ −

S N **READING THE TAPE** N S

n the magnetized spot passes the 'read' head a voltage is induced in its coil, in one
tion or the other. Thus a '1' or '0' is read.

Operation of Magnetic Tape Unit

Magnetic tape can be used for input, output or for storing data. It can carry up to a maximum of nine rows of magnetic spots, each row, or *track*, having its own reading/writing heads for playing back or recording the information. The tape is run from one reel onto another, not continuously, but as the information is required for processing within the computer. It is therefore important that an accurate stop/start arrangement is provided, and this is usually done by means of a constantly rotating drive capstan and a pivoting pinch roller (see illustration). The tape cannot be read or written on until it has reached full running speed. For this reason, the information is not written in one long, continuous stream but in *blocks*, with a space between each block to allow a stopping and starting interval. This space, known as the *inter-block gap*, is approximately one inch long.

The tape driving motors are electrically operated and have very precise arrangements to ensure that the tape runs at a constant speed and that it can be started and stopped in an extremely short time. Actually, acceleration from one inch per second to the normal running speed of one hundred inches per second is usually accomplished in as little as two or three thousandths of a second. Slowing down and stopping takes the same time.

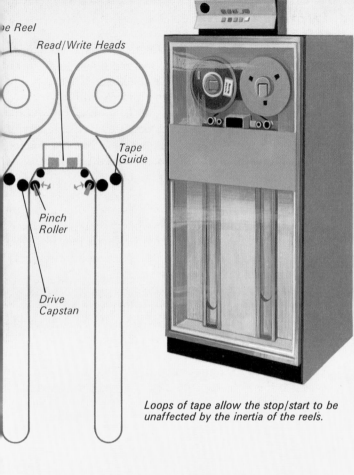

e Reel

Read/Write Heads

Tape Guide

Pinch Roller

Drive Capstan

Loops of tape allow the stop/start to be unaffected by the inertia of the reels.

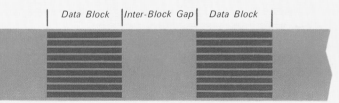

Data Block	Inter-Block Gap	Data Block

9 TRACK MAGNETIC TAPE

'Writing' the Code

Electrical pulses produced by the reading mechanism of the computer are next 'written down'—not with pen or pencil as we normally understand writing, but electrically. That is to say, the information represented by the pulses is recorded and held in a register or electrical store until it is needed for a calculation or other purpose. In a way this is rather like the human memory in which information is stored up ready to be brought forward when it is required.

We have seen that a suitable code for a digital computer uses only two pieces of information, namely a 'pulse' or 'no-pulse'. Such information is called *binary* (see page 36) and can be represented by numbers. For example, 'pulse' = 1, 'no-pulse' = 0.

The diagram on the page opposite illustrates how such information can be transferred from the reading mechanism to a register. A shift register is shown—so called because the arrival of the first pulse (or no-pulse) causes the information already stored to move one place to the right—in this case the register was initially empty. A vacant position occurs at the extreme left hand end and the pulse which triggered the move right is stored there. The process is repeated each time a pulse (or no-pulse) arrives, until the whole register is full.

From the previous chapter we know that 'reading' is taking the coded information from punched cards or paper tape. 'Writing' is recording this information and storing it away for future use.

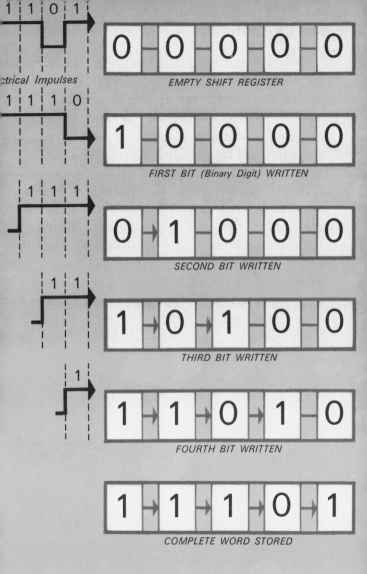

Electrical Impulses

EMPTY SHIFT REGISTER

FIRST BIT (Binary Digit) WRITTEN

SECOND BIT WRITTEN

THIRD BIT WRITTEN

FOURTH BIT WRITTEN

COMPLETE WORD STORED

THE WORD '11101' WRITTEN AND STORED IN A
SHIFT REGISTER

The Computer Store

Human beings cannot remember everything that enters their brains and their general knowledge is limited. But they are able to refer to books of various kinds to find the information they need. These books are stores of information, often contained in a library where they can be referred to from time to time.

One of the most important features of a modern computer system is its ability to hold a vast amount of information which can be drawn upon when required. The registers, we know, are small working stores used mostly for arithmetic calculations and have a very limited capacity for storing information. It is therefore necessary to have an extra storage system where alphanumeric information can be held more permanently. The information can be produced, like a book in a library, for processing in the registers and returned to the store when finished with. Out-of-date information can be removed and new data added.

There are several types of storage system in use, most of them magnetic, and we shall be dealing with these in the next few chapters. They each have advantages and disadvantages. Some are more efficient but too expensive for many computer applications. Some have extra large capacity, others are very fast. Generally speaking, computer stores are a compromise between speed, convenience and expense.

MAGNETIC DISC STORE (front)
MAGNETIC TAPE UNIT (rear)

'Words', 'Bits' and 'Addresses'

A computer *word* is an arrangement of binary digits, or *bits*, which have a special meaning to the computer. The number of bits in a word is known as the *word length* and may be as many as fifty, although this figure will vary according to the design of the computer.

The store of the central processor can contain up to 256,000 words, and it is necessary to select a certain number of these for use in a particular calculation. It is vitally important, therefore, that their exact positions are known, otherwise the calculation could not take place. The store is, in fact, divided up into compartments, or *locations*. Each location holds a word and its position is identified by a serial number known as the *address*.

Computer words are of two types: *instruction words* which tell the computer what to do, and *data words* which represent the numbers the computer has to use in its calculations. An instruction word has itself got two parts: the first part is the operation code, or *op. code*, which describes in number form the operation to be performed. The second part contains one or more addresses of data words with which the computer is to carry out its arithmetic. The number of addresses required for a particular calculation may vary between one and three but is more usually one or two. The tables opposite show how information may be contained in instruction words for the different systems.

INSTRUCTION

Operation Code	Address 1	Address 2	Address 3

← 1 word →

THREE-ADDRESS SYSTEM

OP. CODE	The operation to be executed by the computer
ADDRESS 1	The address of the first piece of data
ADDRESS 2	The address of the second piece of data
ADDRESS 3	The address into which result should be placed

TWO-ADDRESS SYSTEM

OP. CODE	The operation to be executed by the computer
ADDRESS 1	The address of the first piece of data
ADDRESS 2	The address of the second piece of data

ONE-ADDRESS SYSTEM

OP. CODE	The operation to be executed by the computer
ADDRESS	The address of the data

The Magnetic Core Store

The calculating speed of a computer depends on the time needed to select and take two numbers from a store and return the result of the calculation to it. What we must therefore have is the fastest possible access time.

A widely-used type of high-speed store, particularly for the computer's central processor, employs *ferrite* rings. These are very small rings of a ceramic material which can be magnetized. Each ring, about the size of a typewriter 'o', is known as a *core* and is capable of being magnetized in one of two states in order to represent either a binary 1 or 0. The cores are threaded on to wire grids at the point where the wires cross. The change from one state to the other of any one core—called 'switching'—can only be brought about by passing a pulse of current along each of the two wires which link that core uniquely. A third wire—called the sense wire—is used to read the information stored.

In a fairly big computer installation there may be over a million cores but switching takes place so quickly that information can be selected from, and replaced in, any particular core in about one millionth of a second. Because any word in the store can be reached in an equal time, *magnetic core stores* are often known as *random access stores* and computers using them are sometimes able to make nearly a million additions every second.

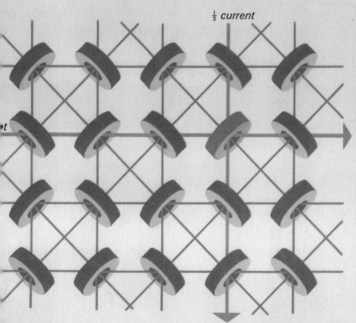

Ferrite Ring or Core

MAGNETIZING A CORE

A pulse of current magnetizes the core. Binary 1 is written.
When the pulse is removed the magnetism remains.
A pulse in the opposite direction reverses the cores magnetic state.
Binary 0 is written.

(a)   (b)   (c)

½ current

PART OF A MAGNETIC CORE STORE

If the current needed to switch a core is passed through a horizontal and vertical wire, only the core at the intersection of the wires receiving full current. By this means any core may be switched without affecting the remainder. The diagonal 'sense' wires are used when reading.

'Gates' and 'Highways'

To understand how a computer works when moving numbers around the central processor, we must try to think in terms of short electrical pulses, each lasting for about one millionth of a second and following each other like bullets out of a machine gun, but many thousands of times faster. The wires along which the pulses travel between one register and another are commonly known as *highways* and the electronic switches which can be opened to admit a pulse, or closed to block it off, are known as *gates*.

Numbers, represented by the pattern of pulses and no-pulses, are sent speeding along the highways and the appropriate gates are opened or closed as necessary to admit them or block them off. For example in the diagram opposite, numbers from any two of the three registers, A, B and C, can be sent down the highways leading to the adder and the resulting sum returned to A, B or C.

This example shows that by controlling the time for which a group of gates are opened it is possible to form many different routes in the computer in a fraction of a second. The calculating speed of a computer is determined both by the speed at which information can be selected from the various locations and by the speed with which the routes can be set up.

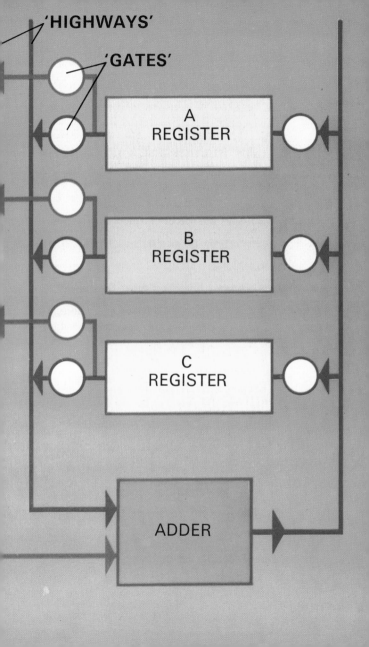

Computer Arithmetic

The electronic circuits used in a computer are arranged so that the coded pattern on the input cards or tape can be used to perform arithmetic—done in a special unit called the *arithmetic unit*. Before describing how it does this, let us see what sort of arithmetic we require the computer to do. It is possible to perform very long and complicated calculations by breaking them down into a number of simple calculations strung together in the right order to give the final answer. Addition, subtraction, multiplication and division are the arithmetic operations used most frequently, and so the arithmetic unit is designed to do just these.

Those readers who have seen or used a hand calculating machine will remember that turning the handle clockwise adds the number in one register to the contents of another, while turning it anti-clockwise subtracts the two numbers. Numbers in a register can also be shifted to the left or to the right by means of another handle. In this way multiplication and division can be performed. The circuits in the arithmetic unit do the same job but work, of course, very many times faster than our hand calculating machine.

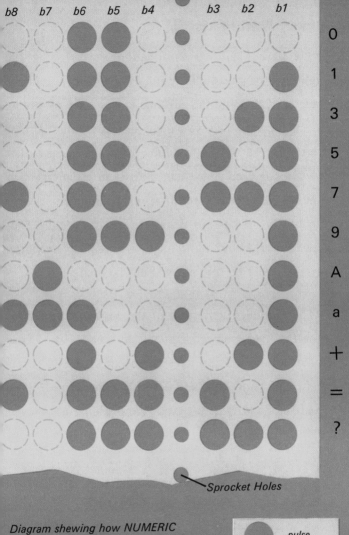

b8	b7	b6	b5	b4		b3	b2	b1	
		●	●		●				0
●		●	●		●			●	1
		●	●		●		●	●	3
			●		●	●		●	5
●			●		●	●	●	●	7
		●	●	●	●			●	9
	●				●			●	A
●	●				●			●	a
		●			●		●	●	+
●		●	●		●	●		●	=
		●	●	●	●	●	●	●	?

Sprocket Holes

Diagram shewing how NUMERIC and ALPHABETIC data is coded on 8-hole punched paper tape before entering the store and being used in the ARITHMETIC UNIT.

● pulse

◌ no pulse

Binary Arithmetic

We have seen that information travels along the highways as pulses or no-pulses. If we call each of these a *digit* then the arithmetic unit has to do its arithmetic with only two digits instead of the ten that we use for our own calculations. The system using ten digits is the decimal system, the system using only two digits is called the *binary system*. The numbers used in the binary system are 0 and 1, so that a pulse can represent a 1 and a no-pulse a 0 (equally well the reverse would be true but will not be used).

The examples at the top of the page opposite show how the two number systems are made up. Those students who already have some knowledge of arithmetic will know that addition and subtraction follow fixed rules and that two tables can be built up, one for addition and one for subtraction, which will give the answer for any two digits which we wish to add or subtract. For binary arithmetic there are four entries in each table, as shown opposite. Keeping an eye on these tables will help when following the examples given of binary addition and subtraction.

EXAMPLES OF COMPUTER ARITHMETIC

A Decimal number is written:

$$5638 \equiv \boxed{5 \times 1000} + \boxed{6 \times 100} + \boxed{3 \times 10} + \boxed{8 \times 1}$$

$$\equiv \boxed{5 \times 10^3} + \boxed{6 \times 10^2} + \boxed{3 \times 10^1} + \boxed{8 \times 10^0}$$

A Binary number is written:

$$1101 \equiv \boxed{1 \times 2^3} + \boxed{1 \times 2^2} + \boxed{0 \times 2^1} + \boxed{1 \times 2^0}$$

$$\equiv \boxed{1 \times 8} + \boxed{1 \times 4} + \boxed{0 \times 2} + \boxed{1 \times 1}$$

$$\equiv \boxed{13 \text{ as a decimal number}}$$

Knowing how to translate from Binary to Decimal, together with the tables for addition and subtraction, we can work some examples:

ADDITION TABLE				SUBTRACTION TABLE		
	+ 0	+ 1			+ 1	+ 0
+ 0	0	1		− 0	1	0
+ 1	1	0 + carry 1		− 1	0	1 + borrow 1

	c c			b b
7	0 1 1 1		13	1 1 0 1
+ 6	+ 0 1 1 0		− 7	− 0 1 1 1
13	1 1 0 1		6	0 1 1 0

Programming

A set of instructions given to a computer is known as a *program*. The first step in preparing such a program is to draw a *flow chart*, two examples of which are shown opposite. This is built up from a number of connected boxes, the label attached to each box showing the job or calculation which is to be done at each step. One very important type of box is the *decision box*, in which a question is asked. The only answers allowed to the computer are 'yes' or 'no' and although this may seem too simple to be of use in a complicated problem, remember that a computer can ask nearly half-a-million questions a second!

Transferring the job of each box into number form (*machine code*) is very laborious, and the programmer is helped in this task by an intermediate language (*high level language*) which is then translated by a master program (*the compiler*) into machine code. There are many high level languages in use, the most common being FORTRAN (Formula Translation), ALGOL (Algorithmic Language) and COBOL (Common Business Orientated Language).

Programming in machine code is a job for a highly trained person, whereas programming in a high level language is something most people can do provided they are given time to learn the rules that must be followed.

38

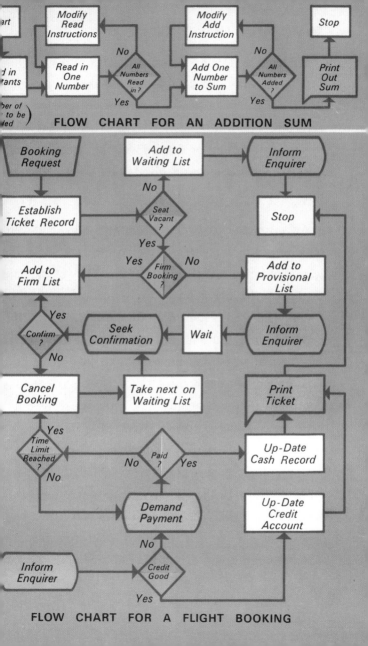

FLOW CHART FOR AN ADDITION SUM

FLOW CHART FOR A FLIGHT BOOKING

The Control Unit

We have seen that a program is a list of instructions kept in the store of a computer. To make this program work, the computer has to look at each instruction in turn and find out what it means. When it has done this the calculation, or data movement, can be carried out. To see the steps involved look at the diagram opposite.

An *instruction* is fetched from the store and kept temporarily in a register in the *control unit*. Both the *operation* to be carried out and the *address* of the data on which the operation is to be made can then be found. The correct sequence of control signals for this code are produced and sent to the gates; these cause the calculation or data movement to take place. The time at which each control signal is sent is carefully controlled by the computer 'clock', which sends out a continuous string of pulses, so keeping all the data movements in step with each other. Meanwhile, the address of the next instruction to be fetched is found by adding $+1$ to the address of the instruction which has just been used. The process then repeats itself, with instructions being first 'analysed', then 'executed' in sequence until the program is complete.

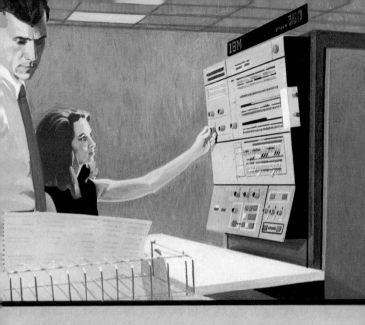

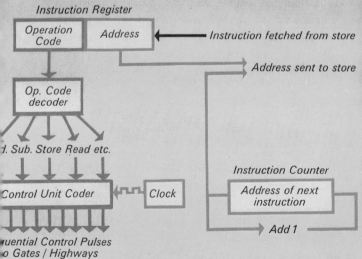

PRINCIPLE OF COMPUTER CONTROL UNIT

Direct Access Stores

1. The Magnetic Drum

Although magnetic tapes are very successful as computer storage devices, they have one big disadvantage. The time it takes to select a particular piece of information, that is the *access time*, can be rather long. This is especially the case if the information required is written near the end of the reel, because the whole preceding length of tape must be run before the wanted item is reached. This can take several minutes instead of a fraction of a second.

Another kind of store with a much shorter access time uses a magnetic drum, or cylinder. The surface of the cylinder is coated with a magnetic material similar to that used on the tapes, and provided with a large number of tracks running parallel with each other around the circumference of the drum. Each track has a separate reading/writing head and a switching system to enable any track to be read or written on.

The drum can be rotated at speeds of up to 6,000 rev./min., which means that one revolution is made in one hundredth of a second. Access to any required item of information is obtained within one revolution of the drum and the longest access time will be one hundredth of a second. This is fast, but still not fast enough for some applications. However, magnetic drum stores are less expensive than some other types and are able to hold a great deal of information in a reasonably small space.

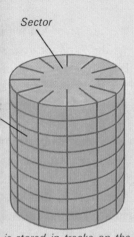

Sector

... is stored in tracks on the drum's
...ce. The data address specifies
...rack and sector in which it is
...ed.

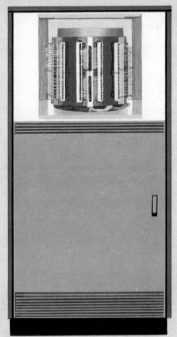

This unit can store up to 3·91 million
characters in 800 tracks.

Magnetic Coating

Drum

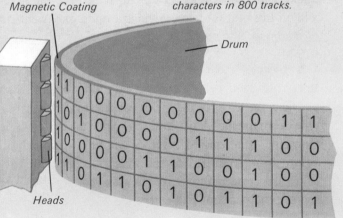

Heads

...he drum coating is magnetized by the head to represent 1 or 0
...s with magnetic tape.

2. The Disc Store

Most computer systems these days are provided with a *direct access store* in addition to the random access core storage. It provides a very large reserve store for information that is not in constant use and therefore does not need quite such a short access time.

Some smaller computers use the magnetic drum system for random access but in the bigger installations a *disc store* is more likely to be employed. This consists of a series of metal discs up to three feet in diameter which continuously rotate on a spindle. The flat surface of each disc is covered with closely-packed tracks of magnetic spots—similar to the grooves on a gramophone record—and they are read or written on by reading/writing heads, mounted on arms which can move radially across the disc to select the required track. Disc stores may have a capacity of a hundred-million bits and the access time is around one twentieth of a second.

A cheaper and even larger form of random access store uses magnetic cards. These are bigger than punched cards and they are packed into magazine-type containers. Any card can be taken from a magazine and passed over a reading/writing head before being returned to the magazine. The capacity of a card store may be five thousand-million bits and access time is about half-a-second.

...ing a disc pack into ...nit.

Disc Storage Unit
using removable disc packs
each capable of storing 7·25 million characters.

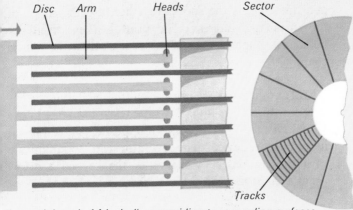

Disc   Arm   Heads   Sector

Tracks

...disc pack has six 14 inch discs providing ten recording surfaces. ...arm assembly moves in and out to give the heads access to the whole ...ding area. Data address specifies disc, sector and track.

The Output Unit

The final part of a computer we should know something about is the *output unit*, which presents the results of the machine's operations in printed or other visual form, or on tapes and discs.

One type of printer is able to print a complete line at a time. Briefly, it consists of a series of 160 revolving wheels which have spaced around their circumference all the letters of the alphabet as well as the decimal numbers. Paper is placed over the type-wheels with a piece of carbon paper between. As the correct characters come into position, a row of electrically-operated hammers strike the paper which then takes an impression of the type.

Another method uses a process known as *Xerography* in which tiny specks of powdered ink are electrostatically drawn toward plastic-coated paper. An electric pulse is passed through the line of type to be printed and this collects the specks together into the shape of the various characters. The print is then 'fixed' by passing through heated rollers which soften the plastic coating.

Still another way we can get output, including graphs and drawings, is as a display on a television screen. The Visual Display Console, shown opposite, is a combined input/output device. The operator can communicate with the computer by means of the keyboard or by using a 'light pen' on the tube face.

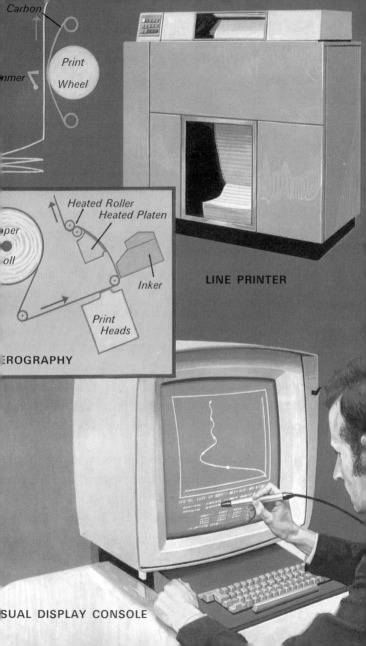

Carbon

Print Wheel

Hammer

LINE PRINTER

Heated Roller
Heated Platen

Paper Roll

Inker

Print Heads

XEROGRAPHY

VISUAL DISPLAY CONSOLE

Does a Computer make Mistakes?

Programmers, being human, are sometimes liable to make mistakes. Computers, being machines, occasionally develop some fault or other. Either way, the final result is not of much use.

Information to be fed into a computer can be checked by a second operator using a machine called a *verifier*. The original punched card (or tape) is put into the machine and, referring to the papers from which the first version was prepared, the checking operator tries to punch out a second version. If the first and second cards agree, the characters are punched out in a *verified card*. If they do not agree, the keyboard locks and the operator has to discover where the fault lies.

A programmer may make a mistake either in writing out the machine code or in a wrong analysis of the situation on which the program was based. Mistakes of this kind are very difficult to trace and the process of tracking them down is known as *de-bugging*.

Finally there exists the possibility of a machine fault. In the input/output devices an additional digit can be added to the code in such a way that an error can be detected. Within the machine, faults can only be detected by running test programs—which check each part of the computer.

OPERATORS PUNCHING AND VERIFYING CARDS
(The punching and verifying machines are identical in appearance)

In one common method of error detection, used in computer storage systems, an extra digit, known as a 'parity bit' is added to each coded character. When the character being stored has an odd number of binary 1's a 1 is added. When it has an even number of 1's a 0 is added. Each time a character is read the number of 1's is sensed and compared with the parity. If they are unlike the error is indicated by an alarm.

CHARACTER	PARITY BIT
1101	1
0101	0
1001	1
error	

This Year, Next Year, Sometime . . . ?

The use of computers is growing year by year and their design is changing almost as quickly. What was up-to-date five years ago may be out-of-date today and what is the latest thing today may be old-hat in five years time.

Apart from their applications in offices, banks, the post office, engineering establishments, airlines and many other fields of operation, computers are now used to control the flight of a spacecraft or supervise the working of a machine-tool. In its commercial and scientific applications, information goes in through the input unit and the calculated result is presented on the output device. Operating in areas such as spacecraft and machine-tools, the computer is working in *real time*, that is, being used to control the actual movement of a vehicle or the cutting edge of a tool.

Computers themselves are continually changing. Electronic valves are no longer used and have been replaced by transistors and diodes which have a low current consumption, greater reliability and much smaller dimensions. Many other items are shrinking in size, and printed circuits are taking the place of wires. As many as thirty components can now be fitted into a capsule approximately one-third of a cubic centimetre in volume. The future will see much more compact machines doing an even greater variety of intricate jobs.

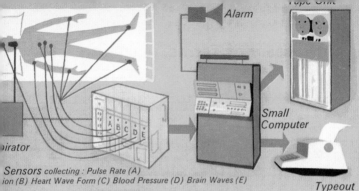

Sensors *collecting : Pulse Rate (A)*
...ion (B) Heart Wave Form (C) Blood Pressure (D) Brain Waves (E)

Alarm

Small Computer

Typeout

...irator

...NSIVE-CARE UNIT CONTROLLED BY COMPUTER
...body functions are monitored by the computer which sounds an alarm at any sign of danger.

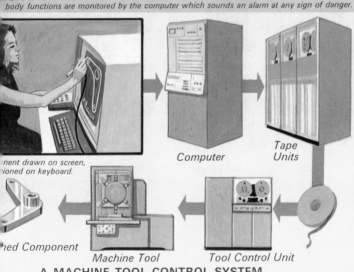

...nent drawn on screen,
...ioned on keyboard.

Computer

Tape Units

...hed Component

Machine Tool

Tool Control Unit

A MACHINE TOOL CONTROL SYSTEM

...ual size

cm

A MICROCIRCUIT

Glossary of Terms

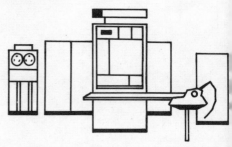

Computers, like many other things, have given rise to their own terminology or jargon, and it is important to distinguish the special meaning of such terms from any more common meaning they may have. The following glossary may, therefore, be helpful for reference.

ADDRESS Computers store numbers and instructions in their store. The store is usually divided into locations each of which holds one number or instruction. Each of these locations is given a designation so that it can be referred to, no matter what number or instruction it happens to contain. This designation is often called the 'address' of the location.

CENTRAL PROCESSOR That part of the computer which does all the calculating.

FLOW DIAGRAM A diagram showing the essential steps in a calculation, in particular the various branches which may occur for different cases.